YOU CAN DO IT!

5

Things You Can Do To
STRENGTHEN
YOUR
MARRIAGE

RON GARWOOD

CONCORDIA PUBLISHING HOUSE • SAINT LOUIS

1   2   3   4   5   6   7   8   9   10   22   21   20   19   18   17   16   15   14   13

Perhaps because marriage seems so natural, nobody deliberately teaches us how to be married. It is rare for any married couple to receive specific instruction on how to conduct themselves in a marriage beyond some cursory premarital counseling. And not only is the counseling brief, but the couple is usually focused on many other things at the time, so the benefit may not be great. Frankly, how many of us even think we need instruction on how to be married? It's pretty simple and natural, right?

Well, no, it is not.

Human beings are sinners by nature, and the essence of sin is rebellion and selfishness. Therefore, all human relationships are difficult to manage and present us with problems. That is especially true in the most intimate of relationships: the joining together of a man and woman in marriage. If we just do what comes naturally in managing our marriage, we can be in for some awkward surprises at best, and some real rough times at worse. So, most Christian married couples truly interested in having a good and blessed marriage usually appreciate some help in learning how.

Marriage has been given to us by God and is meant to be a great blessing to a man and woman, to the community, and indeed to the entire human race. But since we are sinners by nature, having a good and strong marriage does not come naturally. We need to give our marriage good and constant attention and receive guidance for it from our Savior God.

During the life of a marriage, a husband and wife change and mature as individuals, children may come and go, and the world and circumstances are always changing. Having a great marriage takes deliberate attention, hard work, and the grace and power of God from the very beginning of a marriage relationship to the very end of it. A Christian marriage needs focused attention to maintain and strengthen it.

Marriage, as instituted and intended by God, is under direct attack and challenge from the world. In our day and age, many couples completely ignore God's intent and live together without the benefit of marriage. Others rush into marriage but soon divorce, only to enter into another marriage that too often also ends in divorce. Many do not take the marriage union seriously or even treat it with outright disdain. In our country and others, the very definition of marriage as being between one man and one woman is being challenged and defied as homosexuals seek to enter into marriage.

It is, therefore, good for faithful Christians to work to understand marriage as God instituted it and learn how to strengthen their marriages. We should do this in order to stave off attacks against marriage in general and against our own marriages in particular. Married couples should commit to living in strong and faithful marriages as (1) a good witness to the world in regard to marriage, (2) for the blessings a godly marriage brings to a husband and wife, and (3) for the glory of God, who created us male and female and then gave us the institution of marriage.

This book's purpose is to address the strengthening of a marriage in a broad and general way. To do that, five things will be discussed that an individual or couple may do to strengthen their marriage.

1. Remember God's will for you in His institution of marriage.
2. Be in prayer.
3. Communicate with each other.
4. Love each other.
5. Forgive each other.

> [Jesus] answered, "Have you not read that He who created them from the beginning made them male and female, and said, 'Therefore a man shall leave his father and his mother and hold fast to his wife, and the two shall become one flesh'? So they are no longer two but one flesh. What therefore God has joined together, let not man separate." (Matthew 19:4–6)

Marriage is God's institution and provision. So, to strengthen our marriages and have marriage be all that God intended, we will examine what His Word says about marriage and let it be the guide and rule. May God bless you and enable you to strengthen your marriage.

What is marriage? What did God make it to be? To begin strengthening a marriage, answers to these questions are key. Fortunately, there seems to be no shortage of answers, for marriage is the subject of many books. Indeed, marriage, relationships, and human sexuality are extremely popular topics. Most of those books, however, are not helpful because they address these topics in a secular and humanistic manner, uninformed by God and His Word.

God, the Creator of the entire universe, made Adam and Eve as the crown of His creation. In Genesis 1, which summarizes God's entire creating work, we are told, "So God created man in His own image, in the image of God He created him; male and female He created them" (v. 27). This image of God in which Adam and Eve were created was the holiness and perfection of God.

But that holiness and perfection was lost to Adam and Eve and thus to all humankind when Adam ate of the tree from which God had forbidden him to eat. That sin negatively impacted the entire creation, including marriage. However, marriage is God's institution,

"Image" in Hebrew means something that is patterned after something else. Adam was patterned after God's image and likeness, which does not mean that God has a physical body. Rather, Adam and Eve were created righteous, holy, and in a state of bodily perfection.

and His Word is still the norm by which we are to understand and manage our marriages.

Howdy, Partner!

In Genesis 2, God presents a focused record of the creation of man and woman. The creation of man was unique in regard to the rest of creation. Everything except Adam was created by the Word of God. God spoke, and what He called into existence came into existence. "God said, 'Let there be light,' and there was light" (1:3). "And God said, 'Let the waters under the heavens be gathered together into one place, and let dry land appear.' And it was so" (1:9).

But God did not call Adam into existence. Rather, "The LORD God formed the man of dust from the ground and breathed into his nostrils the breath of life, and the man became a living creature" (2:7). The creation of Adam was special and different from the way God accomplished the rest of creation.

Then the Bible states that God planted a garden in Eden and put Adam in the garden to work it and keep it (2:8). At that point, Adam was the only human being in creation, and the Bible states, "Then the LORD God said, 'It is not good that the man should be alone' " (v. 18). God created Adam as a social being, a being made for relationships. Man needed a companion, a helper. God worked through a process to bring to Adam "every beast of the field and every bird of the heavens . . . to see what he would call them" (v. 19). But, in the process, "there was not found a helper fit for him" (v. 20). The Hebrew word translated into English as "fit for him" literally means, "like his opposite." From all the other creatures that God had made, there was not one like Adam, or one with whom Adam could have a relationship of the kind that God intended.

That being the case, God then formed a partner for man from man. "So the LORD God caused a deep sleep to fall upon the man, and while he slept took one of his ribs and closed up its place with flesh. And the rib that the LORD God had taken from the man He made into a woman and brought her to the man" (vv. 21–22). God, in His grace and mercy, created a being with whom Adam could have a unique, special, and intimate relationship.

Note that God did not just create Eve and put her into the garden so that she and Adam could bump into each other. Rather, God, like the father of the bride, brought Eve to Adam and gave her to him. He had brought all the animals to Adam, but there was not one suitable for him as an intimate companion or helper. Now God brought to him Eve, a woman created from the rib of Adam, and Adam responded with a song, saying, "This at last is bone of my bones and flesh of my flesh; she shall be called Woman; because she was taken out of Man" (v. 23).

Adam now had a helper, a companion, who was fit for him, or literally, like his opposite. She is like him, bone of his bone and flesh of his flesh, only different. By calling her

"Woman," Adam identified Eve as the female counterpart of the male. The differences between the man and the woman are wonderful and a great blessing to both of them. As noted from the first chapter of Genesis, human beings are male and female not by some accident of evolution but by God's design and creation. Our maleness and femaleness, our human sexuality, is among the things in God's creation that He pronounced very good. Though sin has corrupted and distorted what God made, nonetheless what He intended for all of His creation is good and positive, including the creation of man and woman and the institution of marriage.

An Invention in Three Parts

Marriage is not an invention of man, but it is God's idea and institution. After God created Eve and brought her to Adam, the Bible states, "Therefore a man shall leave his father and his mother and hold fast to his wife, and they shall become one flesh" (Genesis 2:24). Here God gives us the three components that make up His institution of marriage: leaving, holding fast or cleaving to one another, and being one flesh.

As stated above, sin has caused humankind to corrupt and distort marriage to the extent that it is misunderstood, attacked, and abused. That can and does have a negative impact on Christian marriages. To strengthen their marriage, a Christian husband and wife will do well to regularly study God's Word in regard to the components that make up marriage and His will for us in His creation of us as male and female. Let's take a brief look at each component.

Leave. God's Word states, "A man shall leave his father and his mother." This leaving does not mean the man no longer has a relationship with his parents, but rather it's a leaving of his nuclear family for the purpose of forming of a new one with his wife. The wife, too, leaves her family to be joined with her husband in a new family unit.

The two of them, husband and wife, count all other relationships as secondary to this new union.

No other relationship on earth, whether between close friends or between parent and child, is meant to be the same or as high a priority as the unique relationship God has designed for a husband and a wife.

Hold fast. This new relationship a husband wife enter into is to be permanent. The man is to hold fast to his wife, or to cling or cleave to her. The two will still have relationships with other human beings, but none like the relationship they have with each other in marriage. The husband and wife cling or hold to each other strongly, tightly, in total commitment to each other. They are now to be committed to each other for life. In the Order of Holy Matrimony in *Lutheran Service Book*, the bridegroom is asked to promise in regard to his bride "to love, honor, and keep her in sickness and in health and, forsaking all others, remain united to her alone, so long as you both shall live." In turn, the bride is asked to promise in regard to the groom "to love, honor, and keep him in sickness and in health and, forsaking all others, remain united to him alone, so long as you both shall live" (p. 276).

COMMITMENT: PROMISES AND VOWS

> A person is only as good as his or her word. When someone gives you his word, you expect that to be reliable—that is, after all, the pledge of faithfulness. In all of human discourse, there are few things more reprehensible than a liar. "But as for the cowardly, the faithless, the detestable, as for murderers, the sexually immoral, sorcerers, idolaters, and all liars, their portion will be in the lake that burns with fire and sulfur, which is the second death" (Revelation 21:8–9). In the wedding service the promises are publicly made. The bride and the groom are asked nearly identical questions. . . . Such strong language is indeed necessary because of how lightly many people take these noble words spoken on the day of their wedding. When you stand before God and your invited witnesses, you are making a promise to be faithful to this one person until death, no matter what. Carefully consider what that means. (*United in Christ*, pp. 41–42)

These words of the traditional wedding ceremony reflect the commitment of a husband and wife to hold on to each other, clinging only to each other all of their earthly lives together.

Become one flesh. The third component of marriage described in God's Word is that "they shall become one flesh." This is a reference to the sexual union of husband and wife. As noted earlier, we are created male and female according to God's design. Our sexuality is not an accident but for the purpose of enabling a husband and wife to come together in the intimate union of one flesh. Paul confirms this understanding of becoming one flesh: "Do you not know that he who is joined to a prostitute becomes one body with her? For, as it is written, 'The two will become one flesh' " (1 Corinthians 6:16). So the sexual union of a man and woman is intended for marriage alone, where the two become one flesh as the final component of marriage. Sexual intercourse between a husband and his wife is the consummation of their lifelong commitment to each other in marriage. This one flesh component of marriage is addressed elsewhere in Scripture, and so we will touch on it again in the chapter on communication.

The main feature of all three components of marriage noted in Genesis 2:24 is commitment. God's intent for a man and woman in marriage is that they come together in full and total commitment to each other, a commitment that is so strong that the two become as one. It is a commitment that understands that God created them as male and female, that it is He who instituted marriage, and that it is He who by their commitment to each other joins them together in marriage. Jesus affirms that it is God's intent that in marriage a man and a woman are in a unique, one-flesh union, and He does so by pointing to the Word of God in Genesis 2:24: "Have you not read that he who created them from the beginning made them male and female, and said, 'Therefore a man shall leave his father and his mother and hold fast to his wife, and the two shall become one flesh'? So they are no longer two but one flesh. What therefore God has joined together, let not man separate" (Matthew 19:4–6). Genesis 2:24 is also quoted in Mark 10:7; 1 Corinthians 6:16; and Ephesians 5:31.

So, marriage is God's institution and His creation and is intended to be a wonderful blessing for a husband and wife. That is reflected in the Sixth Commandment: "You shall not commit adultery" (Exodus 20:14), which in turn is commented on by Luther in his Large Catechism.

> By this commandment God wishes to build a hedge round about [Job 1:10] and protect every spouse so that no one trespasses against him or her.

> But this commandment is aimed directly at the state of marriage and gives us an opportunity to speak about it. First, understand and mark well how gloriously God honors and praises this estate. For by His commandment He both approves and guards it. . . . Therefore He also wishes us to honor it [Hebrews 13:4] and to maintain and govern it as a divine and blessed estate because, in the first place, He has instituted it before all others. He created man and woman separately, as is clear [Genesis 1:27]. This was not for lewdness, but so

that they might live together in marriage, be fruitful, bear children, and nourish and train them to honor God [Genesis 1:28; Psalm 128; Proverbs 22:6; Ephesians 6:4].

Therefore, God has also most richly blessed this estate above all others. In addition, He has bestowed on it and wrapped up in it everything in the world, so that this estate might be well and richly provided for. Married life is, therefore, no joke or presumption. It is an excellent thing and a matter of divine seriousness. (Large Catechism I 205–7)

As Luther notes, based on God's Word, marriage is a great gift to us from God and is highly esteemed by Him. Obviously then, it is an institution that should receive our serious and deliberate attention. Not only because God has given commandments concerning it, but also because He has meant it for great blessing, joy, and protection for us.

Marriage, then, stabilizes and protects this relationship because God Himself establishes it as His natural order. This is clearly seen in God's Sixth Commandment where all sexual activity—whether of the heart, of the mind, or of the body is reserved exclusively for a husband and his wife within the bonds of their marriage. (*United in Christ*, p. 39).

So, the study of God's Word in regard to His institution of marriage and His intentions for a husband and his wife should be a regular practice for you and your spouse. The Bible is the best marriage manual ever written, for the creator of man and woman—the One who designed, instituted, values, and esteems marriage highly—writes it. His expectations and intentions for a husband and wife in marriage are revealed in His Word.

Shattered

A husband and wife need God's instruction and guidance in regard to marriage. For when Adam and Eve sinned, one of the first casualties of sin was marriage. In Genesis 2:25, after God created woman and brought her to the man, and after the words of God detailing the components of marriage, it is recorded, "And the man and his wife were both naked and were not ashamed." In their sinless state, Adam and Eve were totally at ease with themselves and with each other. There was no fear or shame between them, no vulnerability or distrust. They were one with each other and with the Lord. It was a beautiful state of comfort, peace, and love.

But when they sinned, "The eyes of both were opened, and they knew that they were naked. And they sewed fig leaves together and made themselves loincloths" (Genesis 3:7). With sin came fear of each other, shame about themselves, a negative self-awareness, and a sense of vulnerability. The oneness they had with each other and with God was shattered. They used fig leaves to cover themselves, literally to hide from each other. And they also hid from God.

In His grace and mercy, God sought them out and provided what they needed. After confronting them with their sin and pronouncing the curse resulting from sin, He promised a Savior. God told Satan that from the seed of the woman would come One who "shall bruise your head, and you shall bruise His heel" (Genesis 3:15). The Bible makes clear that this refers to Christ Jesus and His saving work on our behalf. As Paul wrote to the Church at Galatia, "But when the fullness of time had come, God sent forth His Son, born of woman, born under the law, to redeem those under the law, so that we might receive adoption as sons" (Galatians 4:4–5).

Following the promise of a Savior in Genesis 3:15, all of Scripture is a record of God Himself, in and through the Seed of the woman, working His plan of salvation for sinners and His creation. Throughout God's Word, which is all about the Savior, Jesus, there are references to marriage that offer help and guidance for a husband and wife in living together and strengthening their marriage.

God's Word informs us of what marriage is and should be. We desperately need this help because we are sinners. In addition, since we cannot keep God's Word by our own power, we also need the power that comes through God's Word to hear and follow His Word. For the Holy Spirit, coming through the Word of God, enables a husband and wife to want to strengthen their marriage and live with each other as God intends. We are moved to live as God commands not in order to be saved, but because we are saved. As Christians who are saved through faith by the grace of God for Jesus' sake, we know that God's will for us is always good. Therefore, we know that if we listen to Him in regard to our marriage, we will be blessed.

"He who did not spare His own Son but gave Him up for us all, how will He not also with Him graciously give us all things?" (Romans 8:32). God truly gives us all good things in and through His Son, Jesus Christ. If God cares for us so much that He gave His Son into death and damnation to save us from the guilt of our sin, He will also be concerned about all the areas of our earthly life, including our marriages.

> Adam and Eve lost God's image when they rebelled against Him. God is now restoring His image in those who are forgiven their sins through faith in His Son, Jesus. See Galatians 3:26–28; Colossians 3:9–10.

Ordered by God

God is a God of order, and the Bible states of His Christians and His Church that "all things should be done decently and in order" (1 Corinthians 14:40). In His Word, God outlines His expectations for order in His creation in a number of places and ways. Romans 13 reveals that there is no authority except from God. Therefore, we are admonished to be in submission to the authorities and order that God has instituted. This chapter of God's Word also points out that "whoever resists the authorities resists what God has appointed" (v. 2).

God has appointed order and authority in His creation not to make life difficult for us but to provide structure and security for His people. In fact, the order of creation has its most basic expression in marriage. This order was put in place for husband and wife at the time of the creation, before Adam and Eve fell into sin. Therefore, the order that He has given us for marriage is good and ongoing and is intended for our welfare and blessing.

The roles of the husband and the wife in marriage are ordained by God and reflected in the order of creation. Adam was created first and given a specific place and responsibility in the creation. Eve was created second and in a specific relationship to Adam. God created Adam from the dust of the earth, and Eve was created from Adam, for Adam. Eve is no less human nor less important than Adam, but she and Adam have different places and roles in creation and in marriage.

Relevant to this is Ephesians 5, which begins with a general admonition to all Christians: "Therefore be imitators of God as beloved children. And walk in love, as Christ loved us and gave Himself up for us, a fragrant offering and sacrifice to God" (v. 1). Paul then becomes more specific and moves to the marriage relationship. He first addresses wives: "Wives, submit to your own husbands, as to the Lord. For the husband is the head of the wife even as Christ is the head of the church, His body, and is Himself its Savior. Now as the church submits to Christ, so also wives should submit in everything to their husbands" (vv. 22–24).

Because the verse is usually heard and understood out of context, many modern-day women don't like or even detest Ephesians 5:22–24. God does not intend that women be second-class citizens or that they be slaves to their husbands. Understanding this verse in that way is totally inconsistent with the rest of Scripture. What God intends with His command that wives submit to their husbands is that wife and husband both be blessed in the submission.

Some years ago on a Saturday afternoon in mid-October, a significant college football game was coming on television that I wanted to see very badly. When I announced my intention to watch this game, my wife informed me that there was another program at the same time that she really wanted to see. In order to secure the television for myself at game time, I sort of jokingly quoted from Ephesians 5 that a wife should submit to her husband, and therefore I should get to watch the game. My biblically astute wife then quoted Ephesians 5:25: "Husbands, love your wives, as Christ loved the church and gave Himself up for her." From this Word of God, she reasoned that if I were to love her in the way that Christ loved the Church, I would sacrifice my wants for hers and allow her to watch her program.

In this exchange, my wife rightly understood the meaning of the command of Scripture that a wife should submit to her husband. The submission required is a submission to the love of Christ through her husband. The command to the husband to love his wife as Christ loved the Church and gave himself up for her is a more difficult command than the one to the wife to be in submission to such love. In the order of creation, there are definite roles that husband and wife are to exercise in marriage, and the husband, being head of his wife and family, is to care for his wife and children and love them in a sacrificial, Christlike way. He is to treat his wife as the God-given gift and treasure that she is.

Peter, by the power of the Holy Spirit, wrote, "Wives, be subject to your own husbands" (1 Peter 3:1), but then, as did Paul, he brings a stronger word to husbands, stating, "Likewise, husbands, live with your wives in an understanding way, showing honor to the woman as the weaker vessel, since they are heirs with you of the grace of life" (v. 7). So God moved Peter to record the same commands to both husband and wife as did Paul. Paul, later in Ephesians 5, addresses husbands with more strong words in regard to loving their wives: "Husbands should love their wives as their own bodies. He who loves his wife loves himself" (5:28). This comment by Paul soundly reflects the order of creation and the nature of woman, in that a wife is a husband's other self. For as has been noted already, Eve was created from Adam, for Adam, as his "the-same-but-different helper."

No Christian wife married to a godly Christian husband need fear or dislike this command of Scripture that wives be in submission to their own husbands. The command is meant for her blessing, for the blessing of her husband, and for good order in the marriage.

Much more could be said about the order of creation and its meaning for a marriage, but that is not the theme or focus of this book. It suffices to say here that the reading and studying of God's Word in regard to God's salvation of sinners and His intent for Christian lives, including His intent for Christian marriage, will bring great blessings to husbands and wives. And if questions or concerns arise as you read and study God's Word, go to your pastor and seek his help and guidance. Your pastor is a servant of the Word, a servant of Christ, and your servant, and he will give you good and informed help.

Before I close this chapter, I should finish the story about my wife and me wanting to watch different television programs at the same time. My wife is a very gracious and loving Christian woman. Though she correctly used Scripture in regard to my obligation as a husband to love her as Christ loved the Church, when I relented and said she could watch her program, she refused the offer and insisted that I watch the game. She even joined me in watching the game. I thanked her for her kindness and her love, and the next day I went out and bought another television just for her.

> Wives, submit to your husbands, as is fitting
> in the Lord. Husbands, love your wives and do
> not be harsh with them. Children, obey your
> parents in everything, for this pleases the Lord.
> Fathers, do not provoke your children, lest they
> become discouraged. Bondslaves, obey in every-
> thing those who are your earthly masters, not by

way of eye-service, as people-pleasers, but with sincerity of heart, fearing the Lord. Whatever you do, work heartily, as for the Lord and not for men, knowing that from the Lord you will receive the inheritance as your reward. You are serving the Lord Christ. (Colossians 3:18–24)

Key Points

● We are God's creation; male and female He created us.

● Marriage is God's institution.

● The Bible is the best marriage manual.

● The study of God's Word will bring strength to a marriage.

● God gives different roles to husbands and wives to provide order in the marriage relationship.

Discussion Questions

1. How are the three components of marriage—leaving, clinging, and becoming one flesh—manifest and apparent in your marriage? What does the expression of these three components look like in your marriage?

2. How deliberate are you about maintaining and nurturing these three components in your marriage? How could you be more deliberate?

3. How did you learn how to be married, and what has been your guide or model for marriage?

4.   How does your marriage measure up against God's Word and His intent for marriage? What needs attention or strengthening in your marriage?

Action Points

1.   Consider your marriage and note any practical questions you have about your relationship. Then take those practical questions to the Bible and see if God indeed addresses your questions. Actually use the Bible as a marriage manual—though, of course, it is far more than this. Keep in mind that the answers or guidance you are looking for may not be addressed directly but may be implied or implicit in God's Word.

2.   Add some Bible passages to your devotions or Bible study that specifically address marriage. Through these God will inform your understanding of His institution of marriage. Make notes to yourself about your discoveries and how you will implement them in your marriage.

We are commanded by God to pray, and He has given us great promises in regard to prayer. Therefore, in this chapter we'll consider the use of prayer for the purpose of strengthening our marriages. And we pray for the blessing of God as we do.

Pray for It All

Jesus taught, "Ask, and it will be given to you; seek, and you will find; knock, and it will be opened to you. For everyone who asks receives, and the one who seeks finds, and to the one who knocks it will be opened" (Matthew 7:7–8). Along with this direct command to pray, we also have Jesus' promise that the prayers of Christians will be heard and answered.

With such a wonderful command and promise by Jesus, why would a Christian husband and wife not regularly pray about all things, including their marriage? God's commands are always good for us, and His promises are absolutely true. If we want to strengthen our marriages, being in prayer about them would seem to be a no-brainer. However, as sinners, we tend to neglect the obvious when it comes to God's Word and promises, so we need God's Word and Spirit to inform, remind, and move us about the things that are good for us, such as prayer.

God in His grace and mercy wants us to pray because it is good for us. Prayer is an exercise of faith and an act of worship. Proper Christian prayer pleases God. Through it a Christian comes humbly to the Lord with appeals and petitions, as well as with words of thanksgiving, all of which admit our helplessness and confess our total dependence upon Him.

Based on the promise of God, we know that God will answer prayer. But we also know that the Lord answers our prayers only by His grace on account of Jesus and according to His perfect will for us. The power of prayer is not in the fact that we pray, nor is it found in the specific way we pray. Rather, the power of prayer is in the command of God that we should pray and in His promise to hear and answer our prayers. It is important for proper Christian prayer that we keep in mind that the power of prayer is in no way located in us! The power of prayer is alone in our gracious God, Father, Son, and Holy Spirit, who commands us to pray, for He longs to have mercy upon us and to help and bless us.

Christians should pray in regard to all things, including their marriages. The prayers of a Christian couple in and for their marriage should not be made just now and then, but often, for the Bible urges Christians to "pray without ceasing" (1 Thessalonians 5:17).

The encouragement to be frequent or even constant in prayer is reflected in Jesus' teaching that we should ask, seek, and knock. Those verbs are present imperatives in the Greek, indicating not an incidental act, but protracted action. The teaching of Jesus is literally that we are to ask and keep on asking, seek and keep on seeking, and knock and keep on knocking. Prayer should be a constant and persistent activity for Christians, and therefore must be a part of our relationships if we want to strengthen our marriages. But, from a practical perspective, what does that mean? How and for what should we pray in regard to our marriages?

Pray for Each Other

To begin, a husband and wife should pray for each other on a daily basis. Such prayer may have several dimensions. First, you should thank God daily for your spouse. As noted earlier, having a husband or wife and being joined together in a Christ-centered marriage is a wonderful gift, and we should thank God regularly for this blessing. As a side blessing, as you thank God for your wife or husband, you are reminding yourself that you are indeed blessed with your spouse and marriage, and that reminder is good for the strengthening of your marriage.

In addition to thanking God on a regular basis for your spouse, you should also pray for him or her. Your prayers will obviously ask God for good health and safekeeping for your spouse, as well as any other specific blessing he or she may need in this life. However, our prayers for him or her should also include spiritual blessings. If your spouse is not a Christian, or not what you consider a strong Christian, your prayer should be for a huge measure of the Holy Spirit for your spouse, that the Lord will move him or her to a strong and saving faith in Jesus. On the other hand, if your spouse is a strong and faithful Christian, you can pray for his or her continued spiritual strength. Being Christians and living your married lives together in Christ is a wonderful blessing.

Therefore, praying for each other in all things, especially for each other's faith, will definitely strengthen a marriage.

Another important practice of prayer for strengthening your marriage is to pray for yourself as a Christian spouse. We are all sinners and therefore capable of doing damage to our marriages, of hurting our spouse, or of not giving proper attention to important features of our marriages. Therefore, we should ask the Lord to forgive us for our failures in not being good and proper spouses, and ask that He bless us and enable us to be God-pleasing husbands or wives. Such a prayer is powerful in strengthening our marriages, for God wants us to pray, to beg Him for help, and to be a good husband or wife. The Lord will answer according to His perfect will and wisdom and in His time. He will answer us our prayers and bless us according to His grace and mercy.

Just as it is important to pray for yourself to be a good and proper Christian wife or husband, you should also pray the same for your spouse, that he or she be a faithful and godly spouse. If you feel that there is a problem in your marriage, or if there is something about your spouse that concerns you, carry that to the Lord in prayer. And remember to be frequent and persistent with your prayer.

A young woman came to me as her pastor a number of years ago and complained that her husband, in her terms, was being a jerk. She then related some of his behaviors that especially bothered her. I agreed that the behaviors she described were not consistent with being a loving Christian husband.

However, as soon as I agreed, she became defensive of her husband and began making excuses for him. While she was bothered by her husband's behavior, it was apparent that she loved him and was not comfortable with anyone speaking negatively about him, even her pastor. I mentioned this and affirmed her in her love for and protection of her husband. In that she truly loved her husband and cherished her marriage, we began to discuss what she could do to strengthen her marriage.

First, I asked was how often she prayed for her husband and herself in regard to their marriage. Embarrassed, she admitted that she did not often pray for her husband, for their marriage, or for herself to be a good Christian wife. Instead of talking to God, she had been talking to her husband about his behavior, trying to get him to change. Those efforts, however, had not resulted in the changes she wanted, but had only created tension with her husband, which is what had led her in desperation to come to me. I told her I was pleased that she was concerned about her marriage and her husband and that she had brought her concerns to me. I also told her that I did not have the power to change her husband or to strengthen their marriage but that there was One who could and would help if she asked.

We talked about how she could expect God to answer prayers offered in faith in the name of Jesus, emphasizing that the Scripture promises that "The prayer of a righteous person has great power as it is working" (James 5:16). We discussed specifics she should include in her prayer life in regard to herself and her husband, and I encouraged her to fervently and frequently pray for her marriage. I reminded her that she needed to pray that way, not because frequent or fervent prayer are necessary to move God to answer and act, but because that was God's command for us. Moreover, His command was good for her and enabled her to take an active and positive role in strengthening her marriage.

A few weeks later, she excitedly told me of changes in her husband's behavior and that their marriage was indeed becoming stronger, and she thanked me for my help. I reminded her that I had done nothing, that she had carried her concerns to the Lord in prayer, and that it was He who was helping, blessing, and strengthening her marriage. She pledged to never again underestimate the power and blessings of prayer.

To be clear, not everyone who prays for their marriage or spouse experiences such prompt and profound changes and blessings. But it is absolutely true that the prayers of a righteous person, that is a Christian, do have great power. That's true because God promises that He will hear the prayers offered by His Christians, and also because the One to whom we are praying is the Creator and Savior of the world. As such, He can do anything, and He will, but as He pleases and as He knows best.

At the least—and it is no small thing—God uses our prayers to make us aware of the blessings He has already given and continues to bestow.

Pray Together

Another way that prayer can and will strengthen a marriage is by husband and wife praying together. Joint prayer routinely takes place in a Christian home before mealtimes as we give thanks for the blessings of food upon our table. However, prayer at mealtime can also be a time to thank God for His many other blessings, including spouse and marriage. Giving thanks for your spouse and marriage and asking the Lord's continued blessing in your regular prayers will strengthen your marriage. In addition, if there are children in the home, it is a blessing for them to hear their parents praying thanks to God for each other and their marriage. Such prayers are a good witness for children in regard to what marriage is and how a married couple should pray for each other.

Morning or evening devotions are also a great time for prayer together as husband and wife. When you take time to pray together for special needs of the family and your marriage, you are going to the right place for help. Attending worship regularly and going to Bible study as a couple is a great blessing for marriage as well. Going regularly to Holy Communion together to receive the true body and blood of Christ for the forgiveness of sins is a source of strength and blessing for husband and wife individually and, therefore, results in blessings for a marriage.

There are many opportunities for a couple to pray together. You can name many, many more opportunities or occasions than are mentioned here. Take advantage of those times, and pray fervently and frequently for yourself, your spouse, and your marriage.

Prayer is a mighty tool for strengthening your marriage. In his Letter to the Romans, Paul gave wonderful advice about Christian living in general, which is also excellent advice for those wanting to strengthen their marriages. He wrote, "Let love be genuine. Abhor what is evil; hold fast to what is good. Love one another with brotherly affection. Outdo one another in showing honor. Do not be slothful in zeal, be fervent in spirit, serve the Lord. Rejoice in hope, be patient in tribulation, be constant in prayer" (12:9–12).

Key Points

- Christian prayer is not an option but is commanded by God.
- Christian prayer is to be frequent and persistent.
- The prayer of a Christian is effectual because God is the one who acts through prayer.
- Prayer will aid in strengthening your marriage.
- Praying together is especially beneficial for a husband and wife.

Discussion Questions

1. How actively do you pray in general, and how often do you pray for each other and for your marriage?

2. Is there something for which your spouse would like you to pray? How often do you ask your husband or wife to pray for something specific for you, and why is that?

3. Is there something specific that you as husband and wife should pray for in regard to your marriage?
4. What impairs or hinders your prayers as husband and wife, and what can you do to address those things in a positive way?

Action Items

1. Have regular devotions as a family or as a couple, and include marriage in your Bible reading and in prayers. Include your marriage in the regular family prayers, such as at mealtime.

2. Make worship together on Sunday and other times a regular practice, and receive the Sacrament of the Altar together frequently. Talk with each other about what we learn from worship and Bible study so that the Word of God remains before and within us beyond the time of service or study.

3. Celebrate your oneness with each other in marriage and your oneness with each other in Christ as you commune together and receive the body and blood of Christ, and remind each other of this wonderful oneness and the full meaning of it.

4. Christian prayer is effectual, so pray not only for your own marriage, but make a practice of praying for the marriage of your parents, your children, your friends, and others. Pray for God's protection and strengthening of marriage in general in our community and nation.

In the last chapter, we discussed prayer as a way to strengthen a marriage. Prayer is not dialogue with God; it is speaking to God, which He invites and commands us to do in His Word. Communication, on the other hand, is ideally dialogue, talking with each other. At its best, it's an exchange of information between people, either by speaking or writing. And communication is absolutely necessary for maintaining and strengthening a marriage.

From years of leading marriage counseling, I have found that almost 90 percent of problems between a husband and wife are communication based. Because of our old sinful nature, healthy, nurturing, and positive communication is not natural for us. We must work at communicating. In this section, we'll consider true communication as a way to strengthen a marriage.

To begin, note that not all communication is positive and for good. Sometimes people communicate in order to mislead or manipulate. Usually, this is accomplished by lying or speaking only part of the truth. In other cases people communicate to hurt or harm someone. Words are powerful and can indeed wound people badly. These negative forms of communication reflect our old sinful nature and do not strengthen or benefit a marriage.

Fortunately, people also communicate to foster or reach understanding. This is not only good for a marriage, it is, as noted above, absolutely necessary for managing and strengthening a marriage. A husband and wife must speak with each other in order to carry on their lives together. As earlier noted from Genesis 2, God states that it is not good for man to be alone. God has created us as social beings, with a need for other people, and therefore a need to communicate with others. In order to maintain personal relationships with other people, we must share information and feelings with each other, and that is especially true of the close personal relationship of marriage. Therefore, communication, talking with each other, is not an option for a husband and wife; it is necessary in order for them to have a strong marriage.

Quality Communication—and Quantity Too

We must take the time to have meaningful conversations and work at making sure communication, that is, the exchange of information with our spouse for the purpose of understanding, has in fact taken place. So a husband and wife should take time during each day to talk and communicate lovingly and authentically. That may sound easy, but considering busy modern schedules, it is possible for days to go by in a marriage when only the barest from of communication takes place. But to truly communicate, time is necessary, and focused attention is needed. Therefore if we want to strengthen our marriages, we must intentionally make good quality time to communicate, to talk with one another, and to truly exchange information and reach understanding.

One reason why taking the time for quality communication is crucial is that a husband and wife are likely to be quite different from one another. As noted in a previous chapter, when God created woman, she was taken from man and given to man, and Adam declared that she was like him, only different. And those differences are more than just physical. In general, men and women also think differently and experience things differently; they have differing aptitudes for various tasks. Men and women are very different in many important ways.

If a man treats his wife the way he would treat another man, he may be making a big mistake that could be destructive to his marriage. And if a woman treats her husband as she would treat another woman, she, too, might be making a big mistake that could damage her marriage. Men and women sense things differently, see things differently, value things differently, and again are just plain different in many ways.

Even as general differences between men and women are discussed, keep in mind that not every woman is talkative and that not every man is emotionally reserved. While there are common patterns in aptitudes and behaviors among men and women, God created each person as an individual.

The perceived differences between men and woman form the substance of many jokes. These differences are also at the core of many television programs, movies, plays, and songs. The differences between men and woman can be stark and can, therefore, be quite disconcerting, confusing, and even destructive.

But that is not the fault of our creation as male and female.

As we have already said, we should celebrate the differences between the sexes, for they are indeed intended for our good. Woman was created the same as man but different. As man's positive opposite, she was made a helper fit for him. Because God created men and women with wonderful differences so they could complement and complete each other, these differences don't have to result in conflict. In fact, before the fall into sin, the differences between Adam and Eve were not problematic but blessings. It is sin, and our sinful nature, that has made the differences between man and woman the cause of trouble.

For this reason, the Christian husband and wife need good, frequent, and open communication. In order for a man to understand his wife and for a wife to understand her husband, they must communicate, exchanging meaningful information so that understanding is fostered and nurtured.

A Christian husband, understanding that his wife is wonderfully different from himself, should use communication with her as a tool to learn to know and understand her. This can be an interesting, positive, and pleasing adventure. And this is also true for a Christian wife. This joyful task of getting to know your spouse is always ongoing, for about the time you think you've got your husband or wife figured out, he or she changes. A Christian husband and wife are always maturing, learning, growing, and changing as individuals, and so communication together in marriage is always necessary and should be interesting and rewarding.

Deliberate Communication

As already noted, a husband and wife should be deliberate in making time for quality communication. They should look for time in every day to share information about each other's day and to talk about important issues regarding family, church, and work. They should explore each other's feelings about substantive matters and address each other's concerns. In addition to such times in each day, they should arrange for extended time for communication and nurturing of each other and therefore of their marriage.

Some married couples set aside a night each week for a date. They go out for dinner or a movie or some other activity, and in this time together they can talk and share information and emotions with each other on a variety of topics, including each other and their marriage. Another good idea is to plan a weekend together now and then, a time to go away from home, enjoy each other, and communicate in an engaging and interesting way. In short, it is good for a husband and wife to deliberately take the time to talk, share feelings and ideas, express concerns, and get to know each other on a regular basis.

As a further reflection on the differences between men and women—and at the risk of overgeneralizing—taking the time to share information and feelings is relatively easy for many woman. Women tend to be naturally expressive and want to talk and share feelings and discuss concerns. Many men, on the other hand, are not as given to talking and sharing feelings and concerns. They may tend to hold feelings in and may become quiet and pensive when troubled with something.

Unless a husband and wife understand it, this type of difference in communication styles can make things tense. But as you learn to know your spouse and understand his or her attitudes, needs, and nature in regard to communication, you can in love learn to communicate in a way that is comfortable and positive for both husband and wife. And when communication fails between husband and wife, knowing something of the differences between men and women will help husbands and wives forgive each other and be patient as they continue to work at communicating.

Listen Up and Communicate

An important feature of the communication process in a marriage is the art of listening. Listening is hard work and takes a deliberate effort no matter the person speaking or the situation. Our own thoughts, words, and distractions can get in the way too easily. Good listening is not natural due to our old sinful nature, but it can be developed as a skill. When you truly listen to another person who is speaking, that honors the person and shows that you value what he or she says. Most certainly, this is true as you listen to your husband or wife. After all, your spouse is the most important person in your life, the person with whom you are one, your other self. So what he or she has to say must be very important to you, and by really listening, you validate that.

To listen effectively, you must give your total attention to your spouse. You should look at your spouse while he or she speaking to you and not allow yourself to be distracted. You should ask questions to clarify what you think you heard. If necessary, you may want to say back to your spouse what you think you heard just to verify your understanding or to gain clarification. The goal of good communication is to foster understanding, and to understand, you must listen and really hear. True listening is hard work and takes intentional effort.

In general, listening is loving your spouse and treating him or her as the most important person in your life. This is especially true for husbands who need to be focused and patient in listening to their wives. While many women enjoy conversing and use talking to expend emotional energy and find release for various tensions in their life, many men are less communicative. Often, wives would like to talk with their husbands because they feel that they love them and are safe people with who to talk. However, a husband must be careful how he listens and do his best to understand his wife, or he may make some major blunders.

For instance, husbands sometimes stop listening too soon and immediately attempt to address the issue about which their wives are talking. After all, a good husband loves his wife and wants to fix whatever is burdening her. However, in many cases there is no immediate solution or fix to the concern the wife is expressing—and she may well know that. So she may not be talking with her husband in order to have him fix a problem. Rather, she simply wants to vent and needs him to listen. Just being listened to can be a great help and blessing for a wife. So many times the husband just needs to listen patiently, be empathetic when he can, and not try to fix an difficult situation for his wife. Listening attentively shows his love for his wife and makes her feel valued, important, and honored.

Attentive listening in order to gain understanding is truly a gift to our spouses and is a gift that we need to give often in order to strengthen our marriages. Husbands and wives are truly different from one another, and good skills in speaking with each other and in listening to each other are essential to a healthy and vibrant marriage.

Intimate Communication

In speaking of the differences between husband and wife, one of the most obvious ways in which and husband and wife are different is in their physical bodies. And these physical differences are ones that we celebrate. We are male and female by God's design, and it is His intention that we have sexual union in marriage. Becoming one flesh is one of the three components of marriage as outlined in God's Word in Genesis 2:24. A husband and wife are physically compatible for sexual union, created in fact for that purpose. Sexual touching, sexual intercourse, and sexual engagement in general is intended as a great blessing for a husband and wife. Therefore, such sexual activity is a very important feature of marriage and is also an important and intimate way of communicating.

Our sexuality is indeed a gift from God, and though sexual union results in procreation, which is good, positive, and intended by God, the gift of our sexuality is intended for blessings for a husband and wife beyond having children. Sexual appetite, or the need for physical love, was a part of our created human nature before the fall into sin. Our Lutheran Confessions state the following:

> The union of male and female belongs to natural right. Furthermore, a natural right is truly a divine right because it is an ordinance divinely imprinted on nature. Because this right cannot be changed without an extraordinary work of God, the right to contract marriage remains, the natural desire of one sex for the other sex is an ordinance of God in nature, and for this reason is a right. Otherwise, why would both sexes have been created? As it has been said before, we are not speaking of lustful desires, which is sin, but of that desire called physical love. Lustful desire has not removed this physical love from nature, but inflames it, so that now physical love has greater need of a cure. Marriage is necessary not only for the sake of procreation, but also as a cure. These things are clear and so well established that they cannot be disputed. (Apology of the Augsburg Confession XXIII 11–13)

Our desire for sexual union with the opposite sex is a part of our created nature and is good and right. But that desire has been corrupted by sin, just as has all the rest of creation. So the desire can and has become lust. As Paul advises the people of the Church at Corinth, "If they can not exercise self-control, they should marry. For it is better to marry than to burn with passion" (1 Corinthians 7:9). As Scripture teaches, sexual union outside of marriage is sin, the sin of fornication or adultery. Marriage is the only proper place for sexual expression, and the husband and wife should love and serve one another in maintaining a healthy physical love life.

Note, however, that since the fall into sin, doing what comes naturally in the way of sexual expression is usually sinful and can be destructive to a marriage. It is easy for a husband or a wife to be selfish and exploit the other in the sexual union. So a Christian husband and wife will want to work at loving one another physically in an other-centered and selfless way. Remember, sexual union is referred to as physical love. Love should be the focus of our sexual union. When we engage in sexual activity in a loving and caring way for each other, the dividends are rich and fulfilling for both husbands and wives, and our marriages will be strengthened.

As mentioned earlier, sexual activity, culminating in sexual intercourse, is an intimate form of communication. Ideally sexual union is a sharing of one's self with one's spouse. It is a giving to and a receiving from each other in a way that exemplifies and cultivates oneness, our closeness with each other. For there is no other human being with whom we can be so close, so intimate, so free and open, as with our spouses in sexual intercourse.

Managing your sexual life together in marriage according to God's Word in a loving, other-centered manner will indeed strengthen your marriage in a variety of important ways. Sexual intercourse is an intimate form of communication between a husband and wife and an important feature of a healthy and strong marriage. Paul put it this way:

> Because of the temptation to sexual immorality, each man should have his own wife and each woman her own husband. The husband should give to his wife her conjugal rights, and likewise the wife to her husband. For the wife does not have authority over her own body, but the husband does. Likewise the husband does not have authority over his own body, but the wife does. Do not deprive one another, except perhaps by agreement for a limited time, that you may devote yourselves to prayer; but then come together again, so that Satan may not tempt you because of your lack of self-control. (1 Corinthians 7:2–5)

Mind Your Manners

Another way in which communication can strengthen a marriage is for the husband and wife to exercise good manners with each other. As Christians, we usually try to use good manners and be polite to people we meet in the normal routine of life, such as co-workers, the people at church, neighbors, and the like. Having good manners in these situations is a good witness to the Christ in us and fosters good and peaceful relationships. However, because of the familiarity we have with our spouses, we sometimes are not as careful about being polite and respectful with them as we are with others.

The most important person in your life is your spouse. So, if you are going to exercise good manners and be polite and respectful with anyone, it should be your husband or wife first and foremost. When my wife makes a wonderful meal for me, I should thank her for that and praise what was very good. In fact, even if the meal isn't my favorite, thanks should still be given for her labor.

The task might matter to the other person more than to you, and at the least, your husband or wife will not be upset about being thanked for something small if sincere effort was given. When I mow the lawn on a warm summer day, my wife's word of thanks and appreciation for a job well done is exercising good manners on her part and is uplifting for me. When we ask our spouse to do something, it is Christian love to say "please." It is a show of good manners and respect if I open the door for my wife and allow her to enter

It's easy to be polite and grateful to someone when you deeply appreciate what he or she has done. But perhaps it's even more important to show gratitude to your spouse when it doesn't seem like a big deal to you.

a room first. The kindness and respect shown in such acts is not lost on my wife, it is a good witness to others of the love between us, and it honors marriage in general. Such simple words and acts of honor, respect, and appreciation between a husband and wife go a long way in growing and maintaining a strong marriage. The Bible says, "Gracious words are like a honeycomb, sweetness to the soul and health to the body" (Proverbs 16:24).

Getting in Touch

By now it should be apparent that not all communication is verbal. Physical touch is also a very important form of communication between husband and wife. We have already discussed sexual touch, but the touch addressed here is just as critical for a strong marriage. The physical touch that is referenced here is giving your spouse a warm hug, holding his or her hand, putting your arm around your wife or husband, or simply touching his or her arm.

We can communicate a lot with a touch. It is obvious that if we strike another person or in any way hurt someone with our touch, we are communicating negative things to the other person. It is an understatement that such touch is not pleasing to God or good and must be avoided between a husband and wife.

Nevertheless, positive touch has great benefits that go far beyond the energy used to make the touch. Positive, warm, gentle touches can convey deep concern, care, and love. Positive and loving touches can drain away negative energy and tension and thus bring a sense of relief and peace to others.

I recall being called to the emergency room one night by a married couple who were members of my parish. This couple had a teenage son who would not come to church with them, had refused confirmation classes, and had openly rebelled against his parents in regard to church and the Christian faith. That son was the reason they called me to the hospital. He had been in a single-car accident and was being treated in the emergency room for severe injuries. As I prayed with the couple in the waiting room, a doctor came in and informed them that their son had just died.

I hated that situation, because at that moment the world was so out of whack that there were no words of comfort about Jesus and the victory over death that He provides for believers that they didn't already know. As they wept, I knelt on the floor in front of them and put my arms around them—and as we sat there together, my arms around them, I could feel the tension draining from them and the stiffness left their shoulders and backs. No words passed between us, just love through touch, and it was effective.

Such touch is also effective with a husband and wife. Whatever the emotion being experienced—joy, sorrow, fear, confusion, or something else—the warm and loving touch of a husband or wife is very comforting and caring and communicates numerous positive things without a word being spoken.

A husband and wife should look for opportunities to share meaningful touches throughout their day, and by doing so, they will be loving each other, strengthening their marriage, and inviting the other to offer similar gestures in return.

Making Peace

No marriage is perfect. No marriage is without argument and strife. There will be times when your spouse has hurt or angered you and you need to speak with him or her about the matter. In those cases, ask for a convenient time to talk with your spouse. Such a request honors your spouse and makes for a positive and open communication opportunity. Then, when you speak with your spouse about what has hurt or angered you, use "I" messages. That is, avoid making an attack on your spouse with such phrases as "You said/did . . . and you hurt me." Rather, you can take some of the sting out of your words by saying, for example, "When you said/did . . . I felt . . . ."

The use of "I" messages, working to make your speaking as objective as possible, and avoiding the language of attack will help make your communication with your spouse open and helpful.

> The goal of communication with your husband or wife should not be to attack or hurt but to foster understanding.

If your spouse comes to understand how what he or she did hurt you, then there is an opportunity for asking for and granting forgiveness and strengthening your marriage.

And if your spouse is angry or badly upset about something and speaks with you in an emotional way, it is good for you to remain calm and objective as you listen and then to respond in a calm and objective way. If you respond to your spouse in an emotional way with your own anger or fear, then you'll likely trigger a fight. But if you honor your spouse by patiently listening to his or her emotional outburst and then use gentle and understanding words in response, that will go a long way to bringing good resolution to the situation. The Bible says, "A soft answer turns away wrath, but a harsh word stirs up anger" (Proverbs 15:1).

Another important point to remember about communication as husband and wife is that you should deal with stressful matters between yourselves as quickly and decisively as possible. Don't let serious concerns linger between the two of you without resolution. The longer a matter goes unaddressed, the more difficult it is to attend to and handle positively. And the longer the matter festers, the better the chance that Satan can use it to do damage to your relationship. God's Word says, "Be angry and do not sin; do not let the sun go down on your anger, and give no opportunity to the devil" (Ephesians 4:26–27). So one or both of you should take the initiative and use good communication skills to quickly dispose of any matters between you as husband and wife.

In summary, good communication between a husband and wife will help in producing a level of oneness and intimacy that will be refreshing and will strengthen the marriage.

Therefore, it serves a Christian husband and wife well to be attentive to their communication and to work at improving their skills at it on an ongoing basis.

Key Points

- True communication to reach or foster understanding is critically important to a vibrant and strong marriage.

- Men and woman are often very different, and that is reflected in their need for, style of, and appreciation of communication.

- Listening is a major component of effective communication.

- Our sexuality is a gift from God and a very important and intimate form of communication.

- Good manners, deliberate attention, and caring touches can communicate as much as words.

Discussion Questions

1. On a scale of 1 to 10, with 10 as excellent, how well do you truly communicate with each other in your marriage?

2. If you feel that your communication with each other is not a 10, what can you do to improve and move it up on the scale? What would each of you as husband or wife like to see changed in regard to your communication?

3.	Is your oneness of flesh satisfying and fulfilling for each of you as husband and wife? How easy is it for you to discuss your sexual life with each other? Whether easy or difficult, why is that?

4.	How well do you exercise good manners with each other in your marriage? Do you feel honored and respected by your spouse in your marriage? Why or why not?

Action Items

1.	Arrange for private time as husband and wife, maybe going out for dinner at a quiet place, going away for a weekend together, or simply finding some special time at home together, and deliberately talk about your marriage. If you can, and if you are prepared to objectively handle what you hear, ask some pointed questions. Ask how your spouse thinks you are doing as a husband or wife. What is your greatest joy in regard to your marriage? What is your greatest fear in regard to your marriage? What would each of you most like to see change in your marriage?

2.	In the midst of so many inaccurate and damaging portrayals of human sexuality in our world, reading some good, biblically based books on sexual expression in a Christian marriage is very beneficial. One or more of the following may be helpful for you.

The Act of Marriage, *The Beauty of Sexual Love*, by Tim and Beverly LaHaye; *Intended for Pleasure*, by Dr. Ed Wheat and his wife, Gaye; and *The Gift of Sex*, by Clifford and Joyce Penner. These books are not written by Lutheran Christians and so one must be aware of the theology implied in them, but their practical handling of human sexuality is very good. Your pastor might also have good books in this regard that he can recommend for you.

3. If you are having difficulty with any feature of your communication as husband and wife, you need to take action to address it. Get some help. Read and study the Word of God, speak with your pastor about your problem, read a good book on communication, take a class on communication at your local college, or arrange for some credible counseling. Whatever methods you choose, take action to address the matter!

It ought to go without saying that if a husband and wife want to strengthen their marriage, then they need to love each other. But since we are sinners by nature, and knowing that sin leads us to love ourselves rather than others, we do need to be reminded to love each other as husband and wife, and to do so on an ongoing basis.

Studying God's Word is essential to understanding what it means to truly love each other as husband and wife, for if we go with what comes naturally as sinners, we will fail badly and do great damage to our marriages.

We Can Love Because We Have Been Loved

In the thinking of a natural, sinful human being, love is a feeling that a person has for another human being. It usually is a feeling of desire to possess the other person and even exploit him or her. Because of our old sinful nature, we usually love or think of love in terms of getting what we want or need from another person. We tend to feel love only to the extent that the other person is able to serve us or only as long as we can get what we want from the other person. By nature, we do not understand the true meaning of Christian love. So, if we have a goal of strengthening our marriages, we must learn to love each other not according to our old sinful natures but as we are moved and enabled by Christ as His new creations.

Jesus gave all Christians the command to "love one another as I have loved you" (John 15:12). This command surely applies to husband and wife in marriage. The words of Jesus also inform us as to the meaning of His command to love. He commands that we love one another as He has loved us, which is in a giving, sacrificial, and unconditional way. That is reflected in the Greek word *agape* that Jesus uses for love in this command.

Agape love is defined as sacrificial love, a love that gives self for another and doesn't count the cost. It is a love that loves even enemies. That is the love that God has for us in His Son, Jesus Christ. Jesus left the glories of heaven and was conceived by the Holy Spirit and born of the Virgin Mary, a true human being. Jesus became our Brother. And as our Brother, He lived a perfect life in our place (His active obedience), and then, in that He had no sin of His own to pay for, He became *the* sinner in our place. He is the "Lamb of God, who takes away the sin of the world" (John 1:29). Jesus, God in the flesh of man, was made to be sin for us (2 Corinthians 5:21). God charged the guilt of all sinners to Jesus and then punished Him on the cross with a horrible death and damnation in payment for the sin of the world. Jesus suffered the death and hell we deserve in order to fully pay for the guilt of our sin. Though his suffering was horrible, He did all that willingly, by His grace, on account of His love for us even though we do not deserve it. He showed what is called passive obedience by allowing Himself to die for our sake.

Therefore, the command of Jesus that we love one another as He has loved us is a command to love sacrificially, to love with a selfless focus on the other person. It's a command to love in a way that counts the other person as more important than ourselves. Paul put it this way in his Letter to the Philippians, "Do nothing from selfish ambition or conceit, but in humility count others more significant than yourselves. Let each of you look not only to his own interests, but also to the interests of others. Have this mind among yourselves, which is yours in Christ Jesus, who, though He was in the form of God, did not count equality with God a thing to be grasped, but emptied Himself, by taking the form of a servant, being born in the likeness of men. And being found in human form, He humbled himself by becoming obedient to the point of death, even death on a cross" (2:3–8). That is the way Jesus loved us, and His command that we love each other in that way unquestionably applies also to husbands and wives.

Love Deliberately

By the inspiration of the Holy Spirit, Paul writes to husbands, commanding, "Husbands, love your wives, as Christ loved the church and gave Himself up for her" (Ephesians 5:25). In these words, Paul relates the command to love that Jesus made to all Christians, specifically to husbands. It isn't that wives are not included in the command to love as Christ has loved us, for they certainly are. They are to respect and love their husbands and be in submission to them. But it's the husband, as the head of his wife and the representative of Christ in his family, who has the first and heaviest responsibility to love his wife and family in a Christlike way.

All that being true, what does that mean for a husband and wife who want to strengthen their marriage by loving each other? How do a Christian husband and wife love each other in a way that is different from their natural sinful inclinations and therefore makes their love Christlike?

To begin, we need to understand that a Christian husband and wife must love each other all the time, not just when they feel like it. Christian love involves feelings, but it is not primarily a feeling. It does not show Christian love to act in love only when we are having good and positive feelings toward our spouses or when we think our spouses deserves it. Jesus taught, "If you love those who love you, what benefit is that to you? For even sinners love those who love them. . . But love your enemies. . . . Be merciful, even as your Father is merciful" (Luke 6:32; 35–36).

In order for a Christian husband and wife to love as Christ loves them, and thus love in a way that strengthens their marriage, they must love each other intentionally, deliberately, and sacrificially. They must work to love each other all the time, even when they don't feel like it. One of the great blessings for us when we love in that manner is that our deliberate and intentional words and acts of love even when we don't feel love often bring about feelings of love. When we resist ill feelings about our husbands or wives and deliberately act or speak with love for them, by the grace of God and the power of the Holy Spirit working in us, we are often blessed with feelings of love for our spouses. As a practice that will strengthen your marriage by loving your husband or wife, I encourage you to try this exercise. Deliberately act and speak in a loving way toward your spouse the next time you are not feeling love for him or her and see what happens in your own heart and mind in regard to your feelings for your husband or wife. I pray that you—and perhaps even your spouse—will be pleasantly surprised when you try this.

Husband, Love Your Wife

Even though Paul singles out husbands and commands them to love their wives, wives are also to love their husbands as part of Jesus' general command that we are to love one another. In fact, in the chapter of Ephesians in which Paul instructs husbands to love their wives, he writes to both husbands and wives, commanding, "Let each one of you love his wife as himself, and let the wife see that she respects her husband" (5:33). Two points are made in this word of God that are very important to a husband and wife who would like to strengthen their marriage.

The first point has to do with a husband loving his wife as he loves himself. A number of surveys and studies conducted over the years by various entities have revealed that many wives in our nation live in fear of their husbands. Some of them are actually fearful of physical or emotional abuse from their husbands, which is horrible, absolutely contrary to the Word of God, and totally unacceptable. But, many other wives, though not afraid of physical or emotional abuse, are afraid because they don't know what to expect from their husbands. They aren't sure that their husbands love them, or they even fear that their husbands might leave them, not take care of them, or not stay with them in hard times. The list of fears that wives have in regard to their husbands is quite long and disturbing. There are many causes for these fears, but the main cause voiced by wives is the lack of expression of love and care from their husbands.

The section on communication pointed out that men and women are often quite different both in their communication styles and needs. While understandably speaking in a general way, it was noted that many women enjoy talking and love conversation with the important people in their lives. A wife usually enjoys visiting with her husband and, depending on the nature of the conversation, can gain a lot of validation and assurance from him in regard to herself and their marriage. Many men, on the other hand, do not have the same interest in or need for conversation and visiting.

So, husbands who do love their wives but are not naturally inclined to overtly express their love still need to do so often and in different ways. A husband may take for granted that his wife knows that he loves her. He gets busy with a lot of legitimate things in life and may not express his love for his wife, sometimes for a longer period of time than he thinks. Such an absence of verbal affirmation of love or acts of love by her husband can cause a wife to become fearful and uncertain about her marriage. Some men simply don't understand the seriousness of the matter, but for a wife, it can be very serious indeed.

When a husband becomes aware of this need on the part of his wife and of the possible fear she can experience, what should he do to care for his wife and strengthen their marriage? Obviously he needs to express his love for his wife often, and in various ways. A wife loves to hear her husband say, in a serious and sincere way, "I love you." And she loves to hear it often. I know that is true for my wife, and so I try to say "I love you" often. Now and then I will even ask her, "Honey, have I told you yet today that I love you?" And she will almost always say no, not because I haven't told her, but because she wants me to say it again. So a husband should tell his wife often that he loves her.

Of course, a husband can express his love and appreciation for his wife in many other ways than with those direct words. Simply telling her that she looks nice, that he really likes an outfit she is wearing, or that the meal she made was wonderful or giving any such sincere compliment is great affirmation of a husband's love, appreciation, and care. In addition, asking her how she feels, how she slept, or what she thinks about something exhibits a husband's care and concern for his wife This honors her in a way that builds her self-esteem and makes her feel valued and secure in her marriage.

In addition to words of love, acts of love are a great way for a husband to express affection and nurture his wife and his marriage. Little things like holding her hand while walking together, giving her a hug and a kiss at any time, or taking the time to help her with a chore will likely be greatly meaningful and appreciated by a wife. Sometimes I'll whistle at my wife and say, "Wow!" and she will shake her head and act a bit embarrassed, but her warm smile and positive demeanor show how much she appreciates being affirmed as the woman who still commands my attention.

A husband who remembers special occasions and dates also affirms his love and care for his wife. A card and a gift on her birthday, your wedding anniversary, or some other important occasion is meaningful for a wife. And I suggest that you go beyond just signing your name. Take the time to write a loving note in your card, expressing how you feel about her and what she means to you. If you do that, you may very well find that she doesn't throw the notes away after reading them, but keeps them to read again and again.

Don't make loving gestures only on special occasions. A husband can go far in helping his wife feel loved and secure if he takes the time to send her a card, letter, flowers, or other gift on a day that is not special. In fact such an act of love on a day that has no particular significance really helps your wife feel loved and special beyond what you can quantify.

In short, knowing how important loving words and acts of love are to his wife, a husband can strengthen his marriage by giving sincere and positive attention to his wife. As he does these things, he will usually find that his feelings of love and appreciation for his wife are strengthened and enhanced.

Of course, husbands need attention, too, and a wife can love her husband in the same way. Many husbands are known to appreciate small gifts, such as a favorite snack, or to treasure extra hugs and encouragement going into a difficult day at work. A wife's words of admiration and appreciation for her husband and her high regard and respect for him will assure him of her love for him. Her written words of love in a card or letter are always very meaningful to her husband too. When I served as a district president in our church body and was required to do a lot of traveling, I would often open my suitcase in my hotel room and find a note my wife had placed there for me. It might be something short, like "I miss you already," or it might be a card or even a letter. However lengthy or short, the main message was always "I love you," and I always appreciated her words.

Wife, Submit to Your Man's Love

Now, just a quick note to wives in regard to their husband's God-given obligation to love them in a giving, sacrificial, Christlike way. The way a wife receives her husband's love and the way she lives with him and treats him in general has great power to strengthen his will and ability to love her as God commands. In short, she will help her husband love her as he ought if she works hard to conduct herself in the marriage as God commands, in submission to him, and with respect for him.

A wife is not to blame for a husband's lack of Christlike love for her and actions toward her. A husband who fails to treat his wife with love bears the full burden of that sin. However, a Christian wife who can sincerely praise even the smallest kindness from or positive quality in her husband is a woman who is likely to find those good actions and qualities increasing in response.

Please remember that the point has been made earlier that the command for a wife to submit to her husband is literally a command for her to submit to the love of her husband, which in fact will assist her husband in loving her. The full text of the verse commanding her submission to her husband is "Wives, submit to your own husbands, as to the Lord. For the husband is the head of the wife even as Christ is the head of the church, His body, and is Himself its Savior. Now as the church submits to Christ, so also wives should submit in everything to their husbands" (Ephesians 5:22–24). The key therefore to understanding what it means for a wife to submit to her husband is understanding her relationship to Christ. Jesus loves the wife and has given Himself up for her, redeeming her from the guilt of her sin and giving her the gift of everlasting life. As a Christian, one who believes and trusts in Jesus, she now submits to Christ's love, loving Him in return and following His leading and guiding with His Word. She is given the will and ability to do that by the power of the Holy Spirit working in her through the Word of God. She is not able to love Christ and follow His Word and guidance perfectly, and she does not live in Him by her own power or goodness, but rather by His Holy Spirit, and Christ living in her. So, by the Holy Spirit, the wife lives in submission to Christ and His love and forgiveness. She knows that Christ loves her even to the point of sacrificing His life in death and damnation for her.

God's command for a wife to submit to her own husband as she does to her Lord is meant for her well-being and security. God is not demeaning or devaluing the wife by this command, but rather He is loving her and providing good things for her. For a wife to submit to her husband does not mean that she is a second-class citizen or a slave of her husband. It does not mean that she is of less value as a human being than her husband. The wife was created in the image of God, just as her husband was. The wife is fully redeemed in the blood of Christ, just as her husband is. The wife has equal standing in the kingdom of God with her husband.

So with His command for a wife to submit to her own husband, God has given her into the protection, care, and love of her husband. The Lord has provided for a wife to have security and peace through her husband. And that being the case, as has already been noted in this book, the command for the husband to love his wife "as Christ loved the church and gave Himself up for her" (Ephesians 5:25) is a much heavier responsibility than that given to the wife. This is nothing to boast about or to make into a game of which spouse loves the other the most. It is simply the husband's calling. He is to love his wife in a sacrificial, giving, selfless way. And that brings us back to the point that a wife can help her husband do that by submitting to him (Ephesians 5:22) and respecting him (v. 33).

As a Christian wife respects her husband and holds him in high esteem, considering him as a gift from God and as Christ's representative in her marriage, she fosters in him a love for her and a willingness to care for her as he is commanded by God. Sinful husbands, which includes all of us, need this help from their wives. A wife who serves her husband in love as she is loved by God in Christ and gives deference to her husband in their marriage makes her husband's obligation to love her much easier and serves her Lord Christ in the process.

On the other hand, a wife who does not respect and honor her husband and rebels against him in defiance of the Word of God makes her husband's obligation to love her difficult and does great damage to the marriage. If a wife casually rejects her husband's role as her head and will not submit to him—within reason—she is rebelling against the Lord and His Word, which will have very dire consequences in her life and her marriage. If a wife belittles her husband and undermines him in his role as husband or speaks negatively to and about him, making him feel inadequate and small, she will bring great harm to her husband, her marriage, and herself.

An important side note is that headship does not give the husband the right to run roughshod over his wife, and it especially does not give him the right to abuse, abandon, or break his marital vows to her. The wife is to submit to the husband in marriage, but in cases like these, in which the husband has broken the marriage covenant, the husband has abandoned his wife and his right to headship. Though they are not the first or only courses of action, the Bible does makes provision for separation and divorce in these extreme circumstances. There is no biblical command requiring a woman to live in fear of an abusive husband, no matter the reason. Nevertheless, take care not to confuse a difficult marriage with an abusive one. A difficult relationship can be improved; an abusive one is often beyond repair.

Getting back to the main point, though, a Christian wife can strengthen her marriage and be of great help to her husband by loving him, respecting him, and being in submission to his love for her in Christ. That is God's will for her in marriage, and God's commands for us in His Word are always for our good, and if we follow them, we will be blessed, that is, we will be in receipt of His divine favor. Paul brings a good conclusion to these thoughts with these words: "Therefore be imitators of God, as beloved children. And walk in love, as Christ loved us and gave Himself up for us, a fragrant offering and sacrifice to God" (Ephesians 5:1–2).

The words "walk in love, as Christ loved us" brings us to a point of major importance in regard to strengthening our marriage by loving each other. That point is that we are able to love each other only because God first loved us.

". . . Must Love Long Walks Together"

After God created Adam and Eve and gave them to each other in marriage, they did exactly what God told them not to do and ate from the tree of the knowledge of good and evil. With that sin, they brought death and corruption into creation, and their own perfect and holy nature was lost. They were created in the image of God, which is His perfection and holiness. But after they sinned, Scripture states, "When Adam had lived 130 years, he fathered a son in his own likeness, after his image, and named him Seth" (Genesis 5:3). From this word of God we know that the children of Adam and Eve, including all of us, were conceived and born in the image of Adam, that is as sinners. So, all human beings are sinners by nature. As the Bible states, "None is righteous, no, not one; no one understands; no one seeks for God. All have turned aside; together they have become worthless; no one does good, not even one" (Romans 3:10–12). As noted earlier, the essence of sin is selfishness, self-service, self-love, and rebellion against God and our fellow humans. In our natural sinful state, we are not capable of loving God or a fellow human being as God commands. As sinners we are bound up in ourselves and doomed to death and damnation, for as the Bible states, "The wages of sin is death" (Romans 6:23).

But, God in His grace and mercy sent Jesus to be our Savior from sin, death, and hell. Jesus, the very Son of God, became a man. Jesus, out of His love and mercy, came to redeem us from the guilt of our sin and to win for us forgiveness and everlasting life. He did that by suffering our death and damnation on the cross, and then after being crucified, dead, and buried, He arose from the dead. Through Jesus' resurrection, God declared the sins of the entire world forgiven. That forgiveness, given us as a gift on account of Jesus, is received by each individual sinner by faith, by believing and trusting in Jesus as our Savior from sin, death, and hell. And it gets even better because even the faith necessary to receive this forgiveness is a gift of God's grace and mercy. The Bible states, "Faith comes from hearing, and hearing through the word of Christ" (Romans 10:17).

Jesus said that because we are conceived and born in sin, we must be born again, reborn spiritually, in order to really live and enter the kingdom of God. This rebirth comes about through water and the Spirit (John 3:5). Through Baptism and the Word of God, faith is worked in the heart of a sinner, and the sinner, by the faith worked in him or her by the Holy Spirit, receives the forgiveness of sins and the gift of eternal life. God out of His love and mercy has provided for human beings the sacrifice for sin and the gift of salvation. "For God so loved the world, that He gave His only Son, that whoever believes in Him should not perish, but have eternal life" (John 3:16).

The bottom line is that by the grace and mercy of God, on account of Jesus, through faith, sinners are forgiven the guilt of their sin and saved from death and hell. This forgiveness and salvation is delivered to us on a regular basis through God's Means of Grace, that is, through His gifts of Baptism, His Word, and the Lord's Supper. The Holy Spirit, who comes through God's Means of Grace and works faith in us, also works in us as Christians the will and ability to live differently. The Bible says of Christians, "Therefore, if anyone is in Christ, he is a new creation. The old has passed away; behold, the new has come. All this is from God who through Christ reconciled us to Himself" (2 Corinthians 5:17–18). From God Himself, who is love and who has loved us in and through His Son, Jesus Christ, Christians now know what love is. Having redeemed us in the blood of Jesus and made us believers and new people in Christ by the power of the Holy Spirit, God has enabled us to love Him and one another.

This is summarized beautifully by John, who wrote to Christians, saying, "Beloved, let us love one another, for love is from God, and whoever loves has been born of God and knows God. Anyone who does not love does not know God, because God is love. In this the love of God was made manifest among us, that God sent His only Son into the world, so that we might live through Him. In this is love, not that we have loved God but that He loved us and sent His Son to be the propitiation for our sins. Beloved, if God so loved us, we also ought to love one another. . . . If we love one another,

God abides in us and His love is perfected in us" (1 John 4:7–12). Therefore, a Christian husband and wife are able to love each other as God commands, not by their own power, but by the power of the Holy Spirit in them. Christians love because we have been loved and are enabled to love.

Then, when we fail to love God and our spouse as He commands, which happens more often than we would like to admit, God by His grace and Spirit moves us to repent and turn again to the forgiveness we have in Christ. The Holy Spirit, through the Word of God, moves a Christian husband and wife to such repentance and faith on a regular and ongoing basis. The Spirit also enables us, by faith and trust in Christ, to live in the forgiveness of our sins and to seek to amend our sinful lives and live in love. By all this, on an ongoing basis, God strengthens our marriages.

Non-Christians, those who do not truly believe in Jesus or His inerrant Holy Word, fear and distrust the Word of God. This book's introduction noted that our society does not understand marriage as God's institution, and, therefore, it is being abused, misused, abandoned, and generally treated with disdain. That's true because the non-Christian world does not believe in or follow God's Holy Word at any point, including His instruction regarding marriage. This lack of faith and trust in God's Word also leads the non-Christian world to fear and even despise the word of God in regard to wives being in submission to their own husbands and husbands loving their wives as Christ loved the Church. In our natural sinful state of self-service, we don't understand the true nature of love as giving, other-centered, sacrificial, and serving. In our sinful state, we understand love as something that we want, something that serves us, a mechanism by which we gain something. So when the non-Christian world hears the Bible talking about the love of a wife being a love of submission, serving, and respect, and the love of a husband being a love that is unconditional, a love that gives sacrificially, a love that loves and doesn't count the cost, it becomes afraid and rebels against such words and concepts. Non-Christians often fear such words about love because they are afraid that by following such words and doing such things they will be diminished, that they will lose something and be less for it.

Yet, the exact opposite is true—not because I say so, but because that is the promise of God. Jesus taught, "Give, and it will be given to you. Good measure, pressed down, shaken together, running over, will be put into your lap. For with the measure you use it will be measured back to you" (Luke 6:38). Trusting and following the Word and promises of God is always good, because God never commands anything of us that is harmful or bad for us. His love for us is giving, forgiving, sacrificial, and perfect, in His Son, Jesus Christ. This encompasses His commands and promises to us, which are made in that perfect love.

Therefore, if a Christian husband and wife want to strengthen their marriage, they should hear and trust the

Word of our gracious, merciful, and all-powerful God. That Word commands that we love one another as He has loved us. To husbands and wives He specifically says, "Let each [husband] love his wife as himself, and let the wife see that she respects her husband" (Ephesians 5:33). A Christian husband and wife can indeed strengthen their marriage by loving each other as God commands and enables them.

Key Points

● We are to love one another as we have been loved by God in Christ.

● Our love for each other should be deliberate, attentive, and selfless.

● A husband is to love his wife as Christ loved the Church.

● A wife is to submit to the love of her husband and love and respect him.

● We learn what love is and how to love and are empowered to love by God and His love for us through His Word.

Discussion Questions

1. Are you comfortable with God's command that a wife be in submission to her husband and a husband love his wife as Christ loved the Church? Are you sure that you rightly understand God's expectations of you as a husband or wife?

2. How well do you do in conducting your marriage according to God's expectation and command of you as husband or wife?

3. Is there any way you would like your husband or wife to love you differently or more fully?

4. Is your spouse your best friend? Why or why not?

5. How does God's love for you in Jesus Christ impact and inform your love for your spouse on a day-to-day practical basis?

Action Items

1. Deliberately take the time on a regular basis to express your love for your spouse. Speak your love often and look for opportunities to express your love and appreciation in writing.

2. The best book to read in regard to love and loving your spouse is the Bible. Another good book to assist a husband and wife in growing and enhancing their love is *Marriage Is Like Dancing*, by Dr. Richard Eyer (Concordia, 2007). A husband or wife could read the book and be helped in loving his or spouse. Even better, a husband and wife could read the book together and discuss each chapter to learn how to better intentionally love each other and strengthen their marriage.

The last section discussed loving each other as a way to strengthen a marriage. But, based upon the Word of God, we recognize that we are not capable of truly loving one another as God commands except as God enables us. This section will discuss forgiving each other as a way to strengthen our marriages. But forgiving as God intends, like loving as He intends, is impossible unless we are enabled to do so by God. So, let's first consider forgiveness from God's perspective and His forgiveness of us.

Sinners All—Sinners Forgiven

We are all sinners from the moment of conception. Born in the image of Adam, we are sinners by nature. Commenting on Adam's sin and the results for us, the Bible says, "One trespass led to condemnation for all men" (Romans 5:18). As Paul wrote to the Ephesian Christians, we are all born dead in trespass and sin (2:1–2). The penalty for this sin is eternal separation from God in death and damnation.

But God loves us in His Son, Jesus Christ, and has charged the guilt of all our sin to Jesus and then punished Him in our place. Jesus gave His perfect life for us, shedding His blood in full payment for our guilt. Then, after He was dead and buried, Jesus arose from the grave on the third day as He promised He would (Matthew 16:21). In Jesus' resurrection, God pronounced the sin of the world forgiven. On account of Jesus, every sin of every human being was atoned for on the cross and is therefore forgiven. The only sin left that can condemn a sinner to hell is the sin of unbelief. Anyone who does not believe in Jesus and His saving work on our behalf does not have that forgiveness and is lost to death and hell. But all Christians, those who have heard the call of the Gospel, responded by the power of the Holy Spirit through the Word of God, and therefore believe and trust in Jesus, have the forgiveness of all their sins. We no longer live under the condemnation of sin. As the Bible promises, "There is therefore now no condemnation for those who are in Christ Jesus" (Romans 8:1).

So then, as Christians, who are forgiven all our sin, we are to forgive each other as we have been forgiven. The Bible says, "Be kind to one another, tenderhearted, forgiving one another, as God in Christ forgave you" (Ephesians 4:32). These words are spoken to all Christians in general, and so they are most assuredly meant for a Christian husband and wife as well. If a husband and wife want to strengthen their marriage and enjoy the blessings that God intends for marriage, they must each forgive the other. Forgiving each other is not an option but a necessity for those who are in Christ. Moreover, we should forgive each other from two perspectives.

Do I Have to Forgive?

First, we forgive because we have been forgiven. We forgive our spouse when he or she sins against us, but not because we are good and nice people. Rather, we forgive because we are *not* good and nice people. We forgive because we know what it means to be forgiven. We are sinners! We do not love God with all of our heart, mind, soul, and strength as He commands, and we do not love our neighbor as we love our self, as He also commands (Matthew 22:37–39). Jesus taught that the command to love God as well as our fellow human beings is a summary of the entire Law of God. Therefore, by not loving God and our fellow humans as He commands, we are guilty of breaking all of the Law of God. By nature, we are not good and nice people. But we are forgiven all our sin by our gracious and merciful God, on account of Jesus. Therefore, as a husband or wife you must forgive your spouse, not because you are a good person or because of anything in you, but totally because God has forgiven you all your sin.

Second, we forgive others, including our spouses, because they have been forgiven. Your spouse is a human being and therefore a sinner just like you and all other people. But all the sins of your husband or wife have been forgiven by God on account of Jesus.

If God has forgiven your husband or wife, who are you not to? Moreover, you must forgive your spouse when he or she sins against you, because God has forgiven you. And you must forgive your spouse, not because he or she is a good person, but because God has forgiven him or her. As noted above, Christians must forgive one another as we have been forgiven.

> Your Christian spouse is as fully forgiven all his or her sin by God on account of Jesus, as you are. Therefore, you, too, must forgive him or her.

This is summarized by Paul: "Put on then, as God's chosen ones, holy and beloved, compassionate hearts, kindness, humility, meekness, and patience, bearing with one another and, if one has a complaint against another, forgiving each other; as the Lord has forgiven you, so you also must forgive" (Colossians 3:12–13). This is great advice for a Christian husband and wife who want to strengthen their marriage, because forgiving one another brings healing, freedom, and ongoing renewal to a married couple.

Forgiveness of each other in marriage brings healing and freedom. Apologizing to your spouse for something you have said or done that was offensive to him or her is a great step toward healing a rift or dead spot in your relationship. When you admit an error or mistake and ask your spouse for forgiveness, that brings the matter out into the open and allows two Christian people to deal with it and not let it fester or become a cancer in the marriage relationship. On the other hand, if a husband or wife will not confess a wrong to his or her spouse and ask for forgiveness, not only does the matter remain as a barrier in the marriage, but the spouse's trust and confidence in the husband or wife deteriorates, and part of the foundation of the marriage is weakened. So, confessing a sin or wrong against your spouse is positive and healing for your marriage.

Then, when a sin or offense has been confessed by the spouse, the Christian husband or wife must quickly grant forgiveness. The granting of forgiveness sets two prisoners free:

your spouse and yourself. You do indeed free your spouse when he or she asks for forgiveness and you grant it. It is freeing for your spouse when you forgive him or her and give assurance of your love and that all is right between the two of you again. But it is also very freeing for the spouse doing the forgiving, if the forgiveness is sincere. When you truly forgive your husband or wife for a wrong against you, you free yourself from the burden of bearing a grudge or of harboring ill feelings toward your spouse. That can be amazingly healing and refreshing. Not forgiving the offense can burden your life and your marriage for a long time in many ways.

Being Wrong and Forgiving Wrong

When my mother and father had been married seven years, my dad brought home an anniversary gift for my mother. My parents both enjoyed country western music, and an artist named Cliff Carlisle had a song out that both my parents enjoyed, so my father gave my mother that recording for their seventh anniversary. But when Mom opened the gift, the flip side of the recording was showing, and the name of the song she saw was "Seven Years with the Wrong Woman." She immediately took great offense and was confused, hurt, and angry at the same time. She then let my father know how she felt in no uncertain terms. My father, though, sincerely claimed that he had no idea that song was on the flip side of the recording, and he apologized profusely to my mother and asked for her forgiveness. However, she was so emotional that there was no way she was going to forgive him. The sad part is that her unwillingness to forgive him continued long beyond the incident, resulting in a good deal of tension between my parents for some time. In fact, my mother's refusal to forgive my father caused the issue to remain an open wound for years. Whenever my mother would become angry with my father about something, she would invariably bring up the incident of the recording and hit him with that again too. This issue remained a point of contention between my parents for so long that it finally became a family joke. Fortunately, the tension finally drained away in humor. But failing to forgive one's spouse is no joke and can work great harm in a marriage. It is, therefore, essential to a strong and vibrant marriage that a husband and wife forgive one another regularly and sincerely.

Add to this, too, that we should also forgive each other quickly. Don't let the matter linger or leave your spouse hanging—forgive him or her right away. Get the matter out from between the two of you and take away the opportunity for Satan to use the division to harm your marriage.

And this isn't all! Your forgiveness should be spoken. Tell your spouse that you forgive him or her, and if possible take the hand of your spouse, touch his or her arm, or give a hug. Your words of forgiveness will be powerful and healing, and your touch will drain away negative energy and enhance the healing brought by your words.

It is extremely important that once you speak your forgiveness you do not bring up the issue again. When we grant forgiveness to each other, the matter should also be forgotten. Saying that we forgive another person but then bringing up the matter again and again makes our words hollow and makes it clear that we have not forgiven the offense. That keeps the wound open between people and gives Satan a great opportunity to weaken and damage the relationship. So, to strengthen your marriage, when you speak forgiveness to your spouse, resolve to never mention the matter even one more time. Forgive and forget!

Now, we get to a critical point. In addition to speaking forgiveness, a Christian must forgive from the heart. That is, you must fight back the temptation to hang on to your hurt or anger after you have spoken your forgiveness to your spouse. Remember, truly forgiving another can set you free and unburden you. But not truly forgiving another leaves you with a sack of garbage that will only get heavier and do harm to your marriage. Not forgiving another from your heart can harm you spiritually. For if we will not forgive others, our trust and confidence in God's forgiveness of our sin will be shaken and put in jeopardy. Hatred, ill feelings, and a refusal to forgive others is a spiritual cancer. So we must forgive, and do so, as Jesus teaches, from the heart (Matthew 18:35).

> In the parable of the unmerciful servant, this
> miserly servant refuses to grant to a fellow
> servant the same forgiveness granted unto him.
> As a consequence, he is thrown into prison
> until he can pay his while debt, which, since he's

imprisoned, is likely never. Jesus' closing state-ment on this parable is this: "So also my heavenly Father will do to every one of you, if you do not forgive your brother from your heart."

An excellent aid in doing that is to pray for the strength to forgive and forget. We can't rely on our own strength to forgive as we should, so we should beg for the Lord's help to do so.

Another marriage-strengthening feature of forgiveness is to forgive your husband or wife even when he or she has not asked for forgiveness. Usually such a situation occurs when your spouse doesn't realize that he or she has hurt you or sinned against you. In such a case, if the matter is not worth bringing up to your husband or wife, then simply forgive it and forget it. Put the best construction on the words and actions of your spouse, assuming that he or she did not intend to hurt you with what was said or done. You should forgive your spouse from your heart, even though he or she may never know that you were hurt or offended. That is Christlike love and forgiveness and very strengthening for a marriage and your own faith.

On the other hand, if your spouse sins against you and doesn't seem to recognize the sin—especially if it has hap-pened before and was very hurtful for you—then you should address it with your spouse. Seek out a good time to bring the matter up with him or her, and explain what you heard or experienced and how you felt about the matter. Hopefully your husband or wife will understand how he or she has offended or hurt you and then ask forgiveness for the offense. That will give you the opportunity to express your forgiveness, which will be good for both of you and be a blessing for your marriage.

Pray on It

If you are having trouble forgiving your husband or wife for an offense, take the matter to the Lord in prayer. Remember that by nature we are not loving and forgiving and that the only way we can truly forgive is if we are empowered to do so by the Holy Spirit. If you are struggling to truly forgive your spouse, ask God for help. Pray for a willingness to forgive, a true spirit of forgiveness, and the power to forgive and forget. Pray for protection from Satan during your struggle to forgive, and ask for a huge measure of the Holy Spirit to strengthen your faith and your resolve to forgive. And, as always, continue to pray for your spouse. Then, read and study God's Word, for God speaks to you in His Word and brings you not only great information but also His Holy Spirit to assist you in all ways that you need help. Prayer will also surely help you as you work at forgiving your spouse, no matter what the circumstances.

As already noted, forgiveness needs to be a regular practice for a Christian husband and wife, because they are both sinners by nature and far from perfect. Each spouse will sin against the other, sometimes intentionally and at other times unintentionally, and this will cause conflict between them. But as they live together in Christ, they must not let Satan tempt them to view each other as enemies. That is a lie, for all Satan can do is lie. A Christian husband and wife should always work hard at being in love with each other and living that love. The Bible says to all Christians and so also to husbands and wives, "Above all, keep loving one another earnestly, since love covers a multitude of sins" (1 Peter 4:8).

Based on the meaning of the Greek word translated here as "earnestly," the meaning of the command is to love intentionally, to love with intensity or with all of our strength and power. Love, as noted here, is the great priority for Christian living, especially between a husband and wife. As the verse from 1 Peter says, Christians should love explicitly by forgiving one another. The statement that "love covers a multitude of sins" does not mean that by love a person covers his or her own sin. That is not consistent with the rest of Scripture. Only the blood of Christ covers our sin and works forgiveness for us. The meaning of the phrase in 1 Peter 4:8 is that a Christian should love and forgive others on account of Christ and His love for us. Our love for others, prompted by God's love for us in Christ, should cause us to overlook many of the sins of others, to forgive them from our heart, and to defend them from exposure and condemnation because of their sin. In that way, love covers a lot of sins.

The bottom line is that a husband and wife should love and forgive each other not by their own power or based on their own merits, but on account of Jesus and the fact that He first loved and forgave us. A husband and wife living their lives together in Christ, that is by faith in Him by the power of the Holy Spirit, can strengthen their marriage on an ongoing basis by loving and forgiving each other as they have been loved and forgiven.

Key Points

- God has forgiven us all our sin on account of Jesus.

- We are to forgive each other as we have been forgiven.

- Forgiving each other in our marriage brings healing and freedom.

- True forgiveness is from the heart, it's spoken (when possible), and it forgets the sin.

Discussion Questions

1. How difficult is it for you to forgive your spouse, and why?

2. Have you experienced forgiveness from your spouse? If so, was it freeing and healing, and if it was, how was it so?

3. In what ways do a husband's and a wife's forgiveness of each other strengthen a marriage?

4. When it comes to forgiving your spouse, what impact does the fact that God has already forgiven them on account of Jesus have on you and your forgiveness of them?

Action Items

1. Together with your spouse, read Jesus' parable of the unforgiving servant in Matthew 18:21–35. Then discuss what the teaching of Jesus in that parable means for your marriage in a practical way on a day-to-day basis.

2. Ask your spouse if there are any issues that remain unresolved or in need of forgiveness between the two of you. If there are any, work immediately to reach resolution and a state of forgiveness of each other. If there are no unresolved issues between you needing forgiveness, how can you manage your marriage so that forgiveness is asked for and granted on a regular basis in the future?

This book began with the goal of providing a husband and wife, or even an individual, with five things that could be done to strengthen their marriage. Those five things are (1) to remember God's will for you and your marriage, (2) to be in prayer, (3) to communicate with each other, (4) to love each other, and (5) to forgive each other.

The discussion of these five items does not exhaust the things that a Christian husband and wife can do to strengthen their marriage. But there is enough in these five points to enable a Christian couple to truly strengthen their relationship if that is their goal. A Christian husband and wife who work at strengthening their marriage using the five points noted in this book will find that the skills they learn and develop will generate an inertia in their marriage that will keep them growing stronger in their relationship throughout their marriage. These guiding thoughts will even be of great benefit—perhaps in ways beyond your expectations—to a Christian married to a unbelieving spouse, even if your spouse doesn't realize or acknowledge these blessings or God's guidance for your marriage.

However, as Christians, we know that the great power for growing a strong and vibrant marriage does not come from ourselves but from God in and through Jesus. We are God's creation, marriage is His institution, and He is our Savior. Anything good and valuable that we are able to build or have is from Him, and that includes a wonderful and strong marriage. As Jesus taught, "Abide in Me, and I in you. As the branch cannot bear fruit by itself, unless it abides in the vine, neither can you, unless you abide in Me. I am the vine; you are the branches. Whoever abides in Me and I in him, he it is that bears much fruit, for apart from Me you can do nothing" (John 15:4–5).

Jesus is our Savior from sin, and He is also our Lord and King in this life. As we live in Him and abide in His Word, He strengthens us and keep us in the faith through His grace and mercy. We can do nothing outside of Him, but as Paul confesses in the Scripture, "I can do all things through Him who strengthens me" (Philippians 4:13). So, as Christians, we look to Christ for the strength and ability to live our lives in His institution of marriage. And when we fail to live as we should in general and in our marriage, the Holy Spirit moves us to repent and turn again to Christ for forgiveness and res- toration. Our only hope for anything positive in our lives and our marriages is Jesus. He hangs on to us and keeps us in Himself by His Holy Spirit through His Word and Sacraments. A Christian husband and wife will truly be blessed in their marriage by Christ through worship, the study of God's Word, and the regular reception of the Lord's Supper. For it is by and through Jesus that we will be strengthened in our marriage.

> Blessed be the God and Father of our Lord Jesus
> Christ, who has blessed us in Christ with every
> spiritual blessing in the heavenly places, even as He

chose us in Him before the foundation of the world, that we should be holy and blameless before Him. In love He predestined us for adoption as sons through Jesus Christ, according to the purpose of His will, to the praise of His glorious grace, with which He has blessed us in the Beloved. In Him we have redemption through His blood, the forgiveness of our trespasses, according to the riches of His grace, which He lavished upon us. (Ephesians 1:3–8)